# *Inside*

# COLLECTIBLE CARD GAMES

## THOMAS S. OWENS AND
## DIANA STAR HELMER

The Millbrook Press
Brookfield, Connecticut

Photographs and/or cards and products shown in photographs courtesy and © Cactus Game Design, Inc.: p. 8 (Illustrations by Michael Carroll: top left; Michelle Spalding: top right, middle left and right; Steve Guluk: bottom left and right); Columbia Games, Inc.: pp. 11, 100; Decipher, Inc: pp. 13, 89, 95, 100; Mayfair Games, Inc.: pp. 14, 51, 53, 57; Wizards of the Coast, Inc.: pp. 18, 21, 22, 28, 37, 75, 76, 78, 79, 82, 100 (Wizards of the Coast®, Magic: The Gathering™ are trademarks of Wizards of the Coast, Inc. All rights reserved. This book is not endorsed by Wizards of the Coast, Inc.); TSR, Inc.: pp. 32, 33, 113, 122; Steve Jackson Games: p. 40; Precedence Publishing and Upper Deck, Inc.: p. 63; Scrye, Inc. © 1995. All rights reserved: p. 71 (Illustration by Tony DiTerlizzi); COMBO © Century Publishing Company, Evanston, Illinois, 1995. All rights reserved. Sim-City card © Mayfair Games, Inc.: p. 84; Card Sharks, Inc.: pp. 100, 104, 119.

Library of Congress Cataloging-in-Publication Data
Owens, Thomas S.
Inside collectible card games/Thomas S. Owens, Diana Star Helmer.
p. cm
Includes bibliographical references (p. ) and index.
Summary: Describes the growing world of trading card games, profiling some game designers, offering advice on playing the games and customizing card collections, and listing the latest games on the market.
ISBN 1-56294-581-5 (lib. bdg.). —ISBN 0-7613-0025-2 (pbk.)
1. Card games—Collectors and collecting—Juvenile literature.
2. Trading cards—Collectors and collecting—Juvenile literature.
[1. Card games.  2. Trading cards—Collectors and collecting.]
I. Helmer, Diana Star, 1962- .  II. Title.
GV1235.094  1996
795.4'074—dc20  96-979  CIP  AC

# Contents

This book is for anyone who knows
that fun and games are serious business,
but especially the folks at
Grand Slam Cards and Comics
in Marshalltown, Iowa, and
Mayhem Collectibles in Ames, Iowa.

# Chapter

# 1

# FUN AND GAMES

Games stores used to just sell games. Customers had to go somewhere else to learn the games and to play them. Comics shops used to just sell comics. Buyers went somewhere else to imagine their favorite warriors in action.

Since 1994, however, many games and comics shops have changed. Customers in both of these types of stores now may play more than they shop, bringing their own

When you play CCGs, you'll learn more than strategy. The cards by Michelle Spalding offer an art lesson—she created the pictures by computer!

games to the store. Some come to watch local heroes compete around the gaming table.

The games they play are card games, with strategies and scores. But the cards don't have diamonds, hearts, clubs, and spades. These cards have pictures, like comic books do. Some cards show heroes; others reveal villains. Some cards display places where these characters fight. Some give—or take away—a character's power. Like comics, these cards picture unusual worlds. Like comics, these cards can tell stories.

Players don't share the same deck. Everyone brings a personal stack of cards, and every deck is different. Competitors often carry extra cards, switching some cards between games, even putting more in or taking some out. Foes may run to the cash register, buying more cards at the last minute.

People of all ages gather round the gaming tables. There are lots of games to choose from. Some feature comic-book heroes. One game has characters you've seen on TV. Another looks like a fairy tale, with dragons, knights, and sorcerers. This may be why so many kinds of people, from elementary schoolers to adults, can be found playing the games.

## Card Games, New and Improved

Of course, card games aren't new. People have played cards since at least the 1300s. Card games were even brought to America by Columbus's 1492 crew.

Many of today's most familiar card games were written about more than 200 years ago in a still-famous book called *Hoyle's Games* by English lawyer Edmond Hoyle. Hoyle's book tells players exactly how many cards should be in the deck and exactly what kind of cards must be included for each of the old games. Playing a certain game (like *Go Fish*) would be impossible without just the right cards (four sets of all the numbers up to 10, plus jacks, queens, and kings), because each player has to know which cards to look for during the game.

In 1993, however, a new kind of card game appeared that let players choose their own cards. This kind of game might have more than 600 cards in it, but a player would choose a smaller number for every game. In these games, it was perfectly legal—in fact, it was expected—to play a card your opponent had never seen before!

Dixie makes players into Union and Rebel soldiers to reenact the Civil War. Blue and Gray decks are based on the uniform colors of the real Yanks and Rebs. Actual sites, weapons, and people are pictured.

But that was only part of the game. The new card games added another twist: Players couldn't buy all 600 cards at once. They could buy a box of 60; they could buy a pack of 8 cards. They could buy a pack of 16, or even just a single card. But the companies printing the playing cards wouldn't sell all the cards together. Collecting a whole set was like a game itself. When players started trading their doubles for cards that someone else had extras of, trading became a part of that game.

Of course, collecting and trading cards isn't a new idea, either. Baseball cards have been around for more than 100 years, but baseball card collectors usually gather, admire, and then pack their cards safely away, knowing that other collectors would never buy or trade for a bent or otherwise damaged card.

This was what made the new card games unique. For the first time, treasured, collected cards were also played with by their owners. These new two-purpose cards quickly acquired two-purpose names: trading card games, collectible playing cards, customizable card games, gaming cards, or collectible card games (CCGs).

Collectible card games can be purchased in many ways. Starter decks contain enough cards to make one player deck, though the right combination of card types isn't always guaranteed. Booster packs offer eight cards or more. Single cards can be purchased from hobby shops or individual collectors, in person or by mail.

*In* SimCity The Card Game, *real photos of real places challenge players to build a real city.*

BRIDGE

Must be used to upgrade Water or Coast

$1   0   2

TOWNHOUSE

$ 3   4

COMISKY PARK STADIUM

Add 2 to Commercials and 3 to Hotels within 5 blocks. Must be placed adjacent to a Parking Lot.
Must be placed as upgrade of Commercials.

$15   6   4   3

The common thread in all of these names is that each includes the word *game* or *play*. The game is the most important part—the fun.

There's fun in collecting, too. People collect the cards for different reasons. Some people pursue specific cards because those cards help win games. Others want to have a whole set of cards. Some art lovers may collect only the most dazzling cards, or those created by one particular artist. But, no matter why people want the cards, their wanting has made the cards valuable. People are willing to pay a lot of money for just one card in a deck.

Why do so many people place value on these games?

For some, the answer may not have much to do with the cards or even the game. "I like spending time with my son," one player might say, or, "I like making new friends. So many different kinds of people play this game." Teachers or parents may use card games as teaching tools, using gaming cards to show examples of adding, subtracting, calculating percentages, strategy, logic, or even storytelling. But most people like games simply because games are fun.

Collectible card games are two games in one: playing the cards and collecting the cards. Both games depend on the luck of the draw, as well as your skill in playing the hand you've been dealt. Whether you play one game or both, this book will put all the cards on the table regarding the different roles you can play in this hobby.

# Chapter

## 2

# MAKING MAGIC

Scientists and inventors never really discover anything new. They find new ways to think about old things. Any invention is usually some sort of Frankenstein—a lot of old ideas put together in a new way. Collectible card games are Frankensteins, too—and, like the inventor of the monster, the person who invented CCGs is a doctor.

Dr. Richard Garfield, a professor of mathematics, began making his own

*Richard Garfield, the man who made* **Magic***, celebrated the commercial birth of his popular game and his thirtieth birthday in 1993.*

games when he was fifteen years old. Making games was Garfield's hobby; he said games reminded him of math.

"Math is a subject in which students are asked to solve puzzles," he said. "Working through problems sounds like a chore, but that's what a game is. In a game, you are confronted with situations and required to make decisions, for hopefully better results."

In 1991, when Garfield was twenty-eight years old, he took a board game he'd made to a small company called Wizards of the Coast. He hoped they'd publish his game to sell in stores, but the company said Garfield's game was too expensive to make.

"Too expensive" sounded, to Garfield, like a problem. He knew that a problem is often a game in disguise. He decided to play.

Garfield told Wizards of the Coast he could make a cheaper game. Wizards's founder Peter Adkison accepted the offer. Make a cheap game, Adkison said, a game that's easy to learn and easy to carry around and doesn't take hours to play.

Adkison was a game designer himself. He knew games take years to create and test. He probably thought he wouldn't see Garfield again for months.

Garfield was back in two weeks with a card game called *Magic: The Gathering*.

## Solving the Puzzle

Because Garfield had been creating games for so long, he had lots of leftover game parts to use when he started new projects. But, most important, Garfield approached Adkison's challenge like a logical mathematician. Make a cheap, portable game? Cards are easy to tuck in a pocket or purse, and cheaper to make than models or boards. But making a game easy to learn and quick to play proved a more difficult challenge.

When people learn games, they want to start to play right away, not sit and study rule books. Although the rules should be easy to follow, a game must be challenging enough to make people want to play again, to try to do better.

People probably wouldn't want to play a game again if the first round took three hours. Yet, if a game is over in five minutes, players may not feel they are getting a fair chance to win. Games should last long enough to give the players some surprises, saving the biggest surprise—discovering the winner—for last. So games need to move quickly, but not too quickly.

*The most important part of games is the fun—and pictures can be part of the fun.*

Some card games will feature artwork by only one artist. Others, like Magic: The Gathering, offer a variety of artists and styles, appealing to more players and collectors.

Illus. Melissa Benson

Illus. Dan Frazier

Illus. © 1994 Douglas Shuler

Garfield discovered that inventing a quick, easy game takes lots of long, hard work.

He decided to start with the "easy" part. He knew that in winning a game, two things matter most: moving forward, and keeping your opponent from moving forward (so you can finish first and win). That's why Garfield put two numbers on each card in his game. The first number (the attack number) shows the number of points you can use against your opponent. The second number (the defense number) shows how many points your opponent needs to keep you from moving ahead.

Suppose you have a card with the numbers 2/2. Your opponent has a 1/1 card. If you played your card against your opponent's, you would "destroy" your opponent's card—remove it from play—because your first, attack number (2) is more than your opponent's second, defense number (1). Your card would stay in play, because your second, defense number is more than your opponent's attack number.

Now it is your opponent's turn to draw a new card. It's a 2/1 card. Your opponent plays this card against your 2/2 card, taking your card out of play. All of your card's defense points were used up. But your opponent's new card is also "destroyed," because all of its attack strength—the value of 2—was used to destroy your defense.

That part of the game is easy enough to learn. Now Garfield had to make the game hard enough not to become boring.

Garfield put his love of math to work. He figured out how many cards of each strength to put into a game, so that players wouldn't always draw exactly the cards they need. He decided how many cards each player could draw during a turn. He gave different kinds of cards different powers. Some could only attack, which meant they would be destroyed after one use. Some could only defend, which meant the opponent would probably need a lot of points to destroy them.

Some cards needed other cards in order to work, like a lamp needs an electrical outlet. For example, though most cards are 1/1 or 2/2, Garfield also made a 6/4 card. With this strong card, you could take two or more of your opponent's cards out of play! But, to play this card, you'd need to draw six other special cards. You might have only two such cards in your hand. Maybe you'll draw another one on your next turn. But what will your opponent try before then?

Garfield had to give a lot of thought to how the cards would interact. He believed that the attack and defend numbers were especially important, and that the attack numbers had to be more powerful so the game would encourage people to take action, to make something happen—to play!

Winning and losing are important in games, but so is fun. So, just for fun, Garfield put beautiful and weird pictures on his cards. A 7/4 card might feature a fire-breathing dragon. A 2/3 card shows a chubby baby dragon. The cards have names and descriptions that are also beautiful and weird. These wild words and peculiar pictures help make Garfield's game fun to play again and again.

Putting all of these elements together into a workable form took three months, but the game wasn't ready to publish yet. Garfield asked friends of his who also loved games to play his new game and test it. He wanted to be sure that everything really worked the way it worked in his head. "Play-testing" the game, and making changes that improved it, went on for more than a year.

The time spent paid off. In 1993, the surprises and simplicity of *Magic: The Gathering* became the standard that future collectible card games would use as a guide.

# *Chapter*

# 3

# PLAYING MARBLES IN NEPAL

Wizards of the Coast is a company where playing games is business as usual. The people who work there love to take a joke seriously.

After one year of working with Richard Garfield, a Wizards assistant said, "If Dr. Garfield comes to work wearing matching socks, it confuses us greatly."

Dr. Richard Garfield, the person who invented *Magic*, plays games all of the time. He even plays games with himself. The Sock Game started when Garfield wondered: If a person never sorted socks, but grabbed two without looking each day, how often would that person wear a matched pair?

After his co-workers caught on to the game, "I actually had to start throwing back matching socks," Garfield remarked, "because I'd get hassled for wearing them!" No game inventor truly minds when others join in the fun; Garfield just added a new rule. "Now, when I get dressed up, I try—just a little—to have each sock match something else I'm wearing."

## A World of Its Own

Garfield has been playing games without words since his childhood overseas. He remembers playing marbles in Nepal. "I had Nepalese friends I could barely communicate with. But we could play," he said, because they knew the language of the game.

Game enthusiasts can be found all over the world. *Magic: The Gathering* cards were available in French, German, Spanish, Portuguese, and Italian just two years after the game debuted in the United States.

Garfield believes that every game should have its own language, that "a game should be made so that it communicates itself," he said. In other words, games should be logical.

"If a game plays naturally, that means people don't have to look up the rules all of the time. I view games as little worlds with special rules to use to get things done," he said. "The same is true of any subject in school, but especially of math. Setting up a system of rules and working within that frame is integral to math and games."

In a game of checkers, for example, markers can't move in reverse, unless those markers become kings. In mathematical division, small numbers can't be divided by large ones, unless those numbers become decimals.

Although Garfield says "my math degree is really a symptom of my love for games," he finds game inspiration almost everywhere.

"Take biology," Garfield said. "I am thinking about evolutionary games all the time, ecological games based on the biological food chain and the interrelation of the species. For example, if all the rabbits disappear, the foxes will be in trouble. Economics work the same way. I've imagined a game where every player represents a country. We'd trade products, and decide how much each other's money is worth, the way actual countries do. If my country got in trouble, other players might keep working with me, so they wouldn't have to 'waste' all of the money they have from my country."

Garfield's game ideas seem to prove his theory that there is no wasted knowledge. "You may not see the immediate applications of some school subjects," he said, "but there are still a lot of concepts going into your repertoire."

## Games Growing Up

Garfield added to his own repertoire of knowledge as he traveled the world with his family because of his father's job. Born in Philadelphia on June 26, 1963, Garfield lived overseas from the ages of six to twelve, traveling through India and staying awhile in Bangladesh and Nepal.

Upon returning to the United States, Garfield's family settled in Portland, Oregon, where Garfield discovered role-playing games (RPGs). RPG players often create their own versions, or "systems," of favorite games, and Garfield began inventing systems at the age of fifteen. He didn't stop with RPGs.

"At age fifteen, I made a game where two players each design an army of robots and fight the robots against each other," Garfield said. "To me, the most interesting part was the two hours it took to set up the game. You had to decide what the robots would look like. If you had more weapons, you had to have more motor to run the weapons. If you had more motor, you had to have more battery. My friend and I had a lot of fun playing."

Yet, that first robot game is not a game Garfield would try to sell. "There are guideposts to achieving 'playability' in a game. I, personally, am not very interested in a game that is difficult to learn. Difficulty can often be measured by the length of the rules, how long a game takes to play, how much preparation is needed before playing, and the time a player needs to make a decision in the game. Sometimes, there are so many options that players become confused."

Garfield tried to simplify the robot game, while his own life became more complex. Graduating from high school

**Sahuagin**

Swimmer. May attack any realm with a coastline, regardless of its position.

76 of 100

**Zone of Truth**

All players must keep their hands face up on the table until the end of this player's next turn.
(Off/3)

38 of 100

**Pseudodragon**

If played with a wizard champion, the pseudodragon becomes a familiar, remaining with the caster until he is defeated. No event, magic item, spell, or ally's ability can cause it to change sides or be discarded.

74 of 100

*Games of one type, or genre, can influence games of another genre. Locations and creatures from the* Advanced Dungeons & Dragons *role-playing game were adapted to a collectible card game format in* Spellfire.

meant searching for a college with a math department he liked. Finding that college meant moving to Pennsylvania and taking each special class needed to earn first a degree in computer math, then another in combinatorial math.

"I was designing games as a hobby, to relax. I did it for myself, because I enjoyed it," Garfield said. "I did not intend to become a professional game designer." Garfield was sure, as most game designers are, that selling one game would not bring in enough money to let him quit his teaching job. Magic rarely happens in game design, but it happened to Garfield after years of experience and years of play-testing.

"Play-testing completes a game," Garfield believes. "It's just like when you write a paper. Writing helps you understand the subject better. Otherwise, you might miss important parts."

## Ante Up

An important part of collectible card games that Garfield missed—even though he invented a famous CCG—was that the cash value of trading cards sometimes overcomes the cards' other worth.

"I've never been much of a collector myself," he admitted. "My first thought of a trading card game was that every game would be different, because everybody brings half the game." Like a potluck supper, Garfield said, "It's very democratic. In *Magic*, surprises are standard. You'll regularly run across parts of the game you didn't know existed."

Garfield expected that some people would collect his game cards the same way they collected comic books: using the items, but sparingly. To encourage people to play with the cards, Garfield included "playing for ante" in the official rules, though "I was sure it wouldn't be used by many."

Playing for ante (pronounced ANT-ee) means that, before a game begins, each player draws one or two cards from the opposing player's deck. These are the ante cards. Ante cards are set aside and not used in that game. But ante can cost more than the loss of a powerful card during one game. Whoever wins an ante game keeps all of the ante cards. When playing for ante, Garfield said, "If I start out with all common cards, I can still win rare cards.

"I guess playing for ante is a vestige of the days I played marbles in Nepal," said Garfield. (In such games, players often 'lose their marbles.') "I wanted the cards in my game to circulate. I wanted players to learn to use new tools—and not get too attached to their cards.

"Collecting is both good and bad," he said. "A hundred dollar card is bad" because it probably means that the person selling the card is more interested in money than in the game.

"My primary belief was that if the game was fun, people would find the cards valuable," Garfield said. His hope proved true, for, after two years on the market, Garfield observed that "the cards people play with are treasures to them. And that is good."

## The Magic of Magic

Treasure was also in the cards for Wizards of the Coast and other game-making companies. Wizards of the Coast expected that the public would need time to learn about this new game and to learn how to play it. The company expected that their first 10 million cards would take at least six months to sell. The cards were gone in six weeks.

*Inspiration works across artistic genres, too. Magic: The Gathering was a collectible card game before it was a setting for comic books, novels, and magazine short stories.*

Other game makers quickly took note. After *Magic: The Gathering* received top awards from the Game Manufacturers Association (GAMA) in 1994, other companies began developing collectible card games. By the end of 1995, forty CCGs were on the market, according to GAMA president Lee Cerny. People around the world wanted to play. Within two years of its debut, *Magic* appeared in French, Italian, German, Spanish, and Portuguese editions. The issue of special editions and expansions pushed total CCG product count to 100 before the genre was three years old.

**Designers Who Play Together...**
Steve Jackson Games was one of the first companies to get a collectible card game on the market. Like Garfield, game designer Steve Jackson had lots of game ideas just waiting to be rearranged into a new game. *Illuminati: New World Order* was a regular card game (players bought all the cards at once) before it became a CCG. Another bonus was the expert help Jackson's company received from a rival.

"Game design is a very small industry," Garfield said. "Designers tend to know each other—especially if we like each other's work." Garfield both knew and admired Jackson's work, enough to persuade Wizards of the Coast to invest time and money in recreating *Illuminati* from its original card game format into a trading card game.

"I helped play-test," said Garfield. "Play-testing isn't a chore. It's a pleasure." He did not see anything strange in helping a competitor. He explained, "Wizard's attitude is that the game industry pie—the money from people buying games—is very small. If the companies all fight over that one small piece, each of us will get very little."

Over the years, the game industry has relied on hobbyists for steady income. Hobbyists are people who play a game (like chess or *Dungeons & Dragons*) or a variety of games as serious recreation, the way amateur athletes devotedly bowl, jog, or lift weights on the weekends. While a collector may want only one of every card, without ever playing a single game, a hobbyist is a consistent user.

Dana Blankenship, the marketing representative for Steve Jackson Games, explained that the number of people involved in gaming since the mid-1900s has usually stayed at about the same level.

Competition is part of playing games, but not of making games. Steve Jackson, *designer of* Illuminati: New World Order, *helps and gets help from other game designers.*

"People enter the gaming hobby, but those numbers have always been balanced out by those leaving the hobby. But trading card games have perplexed us with the amount of money coming in," she said. New customers seem to have discovered gaming. Casual players, who occasionally play on weekend afternoons, have joined the hobbyists in surprising numbers.

Garfield suspected where these new players came from. "To me," he said, "gaming is the intellectual half of sports. Sports give participants good social interaction and keep them physically fit. Games give participants good social interaction and keep them mentally fit. I think that's what people are looking for."

## Fun Is Serious Business

Games can be "a valuable form of entertainment," Garfield said, but often are not. Too often, Garfield said, the game industry follows trends in movies and books. For example, S*tar Wars* and *Star Trek* films inspired games based on those characters. But because Garfield views games as "little worlds," he also believes a game "suffers if you gear it toward some (other) world. *Magic* was not based on any pre-existing frame of reference. It has a lot of depth because it was built to be a game, not a token of something foreign," he said. And, though Garfield has disliked attempts to model games after books and movies, he agreed to let others model books and comics after his game. "I don't have any idea if movies based on *Magic* would be any good," he said, "but why not try?"

Garfield believes that serious study of games is important. Since he stopped teaching, he has considered it part of his job at Wizards of the Coast to research and define the factors that make a game playable.

"Games and their terms are so misunderstood," Garfield lamented, citing major newspapers and magazines that referred to *Magic* as a role-playing game. "I think it's sad that such a potentially valuable form of entertainment as gaming is so misunderstood."

Garfield said he expected his study of "game criticism" to last his whole career. Yet, he seems to understand instinctively how to play. His life has been full of fun, both the little parts of life, like getting dressed, and the big parts, like getting married.

Garfield proposed to his wife by asking her to play *Magic* one night. They played one hand, then another. Then Garfield laid down a card Lily had never seen before: a specially made, one-of-a-kind card with a picture of a gallant knight. The words read, "Both players win, and the decks are mixed as one."

Who says games can't be taken seriously?

## RPGs, CCGs, and Plain Old-Fashioned Games

Garfield used parts of many of the games he loved in making *Magic: The Gathering.* One of those games was *Cosmic Encounters*, a board game that played like a CCG, with new cards printed each year that could be added to the old game.

He used parts of other card games, parts of the game of marbles, and parts of a game that had been new when Garfield was a high school student in Portland, Oregon.

*Dungeons & Dragons* (D&D) was the first role-playing game ever (players, including Garfield, call these games RPGs). In RPGs, players pretend they are in a world where creatures possess numbered powers to attack or defend. Right away, you'll notice the numbered powers. *Magic* has numbered powers on its cards, too. But this is where the similarity between the two games stops.

Role-playing games require players to "make believe," just like the childhood games of "school" or "house." But the numbered powers make RPGs different because the numbers help solve the game's "problems."

For example, if you were playing "school" as if it were an RPG, you might roll dice to find out what kind of "student" you'd be. You roll for "smartness"—and get a low number! That means the "teacher" will ask you lots of hard questions. Next you roll the dice for "personality"—and it's very high! Maybe your "classmates" will like you so much that they will help you study. In role-playing games, players use numbers and imaginations to tell a story and solve a problem.

"School" would work well as an RPG, because a school needs a leader, the teacher. An RPG always has a leader, called a game master. The game master's job is to give the players a problem to solve and clues on how to solve it. A game master also acts as a referee.

When *Dungeons & Dragons* was new in 1974, it became popular with young people, who often don't have the money to travel and have real adventures. Some adults, who were unfamiliar with RPGs, worried that their kids were wasting time. Some worried that the talk of magic included in the game was antireligious. Worst of all, rumors started in the late 1970s that young D&D players had committed suicide when they confused the game with reality. According to Kevin Fitzpatrick, former president of the Game Manufacturers Association, these rumors were investigated and found to be untrue. But, even decades later, many people still worry about the safety of role-playing games.

This is why some people have wondered if collectible card games are really role-playing games. For example, in the game of *Magic*, the cards are spells that players enchant each other with. The players must be pretending to be wizards, right? That's role-playing, right?

Not necessarily. Casting spells is just the situation of the game. After all, the game of chess has kings, queens, bishops, and pawns that the players command, much like a prime minister would. But no one thinks chess is a role-playing game.

One of the best-selling American games ever is *Monopoly*. Much like real-estate tycoons, players buy game-board "property," then "build" on that land, and require others to "pay rent." But no one thinks *Monopoly* is a role-playing game.

The first feature missing is story-telling. In *Monopoly*, it doesn't matter if your real-estate tycoon can speak well or run fast or is an astronaut on the weekends. All that matters is how you roll the dice. Likewise, in collectible card games, the cards you draw determine the game. But, in RPGs, you gain or lose points by telling a story—maybe about how your hero successfully talked his way out of danger because he ran too slowly to escape.

With board games and with CCGs, you know when the game is done. In *Monopoly*, the game is over when someone runs out of money. In collectible card games, there are point limits that end the game. RPGs have no point limits. They can literally go on forever, if players pick up where they left off.

Finally, CCGs and board games depend a lot on luck. *Monopoly* has a banker, but no one controls your fortune. The banker can't take your "property" just because she feels like it. Neither can your opponent in a CCG, without the proper card. But in RPGs, the game master can use her imagination—and her rules—to control what happens to you. You can never change that in an RPG—but, with collectible card games, you can change your cards before the next game.

Collectible card games have a lot in common with old games and with popular games that many of us know. But the familiar features have been combined in a brand new way, attracting the attention of people who didn't play many games before. Because somebody saw new potential in old games, people are looking at games again, enjoying them in unexpected numbers.

# Chapter

## 4

# DARWIN'S EVOLUTION OF GAMES

If Richard Garfield is the Luke Skywalker of the gaming industry, Darwin Bromley is its Obi Wan Kenobi. Bromley was born just after World War II, a prosperous, happy time for many Americans. The postwar gaming industry gave Americans new ways to spend their leisure time and money. The young Bromley was one of those people.

"I started playing card games like *Go-fish* after dinner with my family," Bromley said, "four brothers, two parents, and two grandparents. We'd play *Bridge* and *Canasta*. We'd play *Hearts* with two decks and eight hands—if two of the same card appeared, the cards would cancel each other."

Playing together taught Bromley and his brother Peter to solve problems together. He and Peter started collecting games as a hobby. Later, Bromley said, "I became a game designer because I wanted to do something on my own."

But Bromley had learned to love more than games at the family card table: He had learned to enjoy playing with others.

"I am the eldest, and Peter is the youngest. We've played and shared games for thirty years. Like anything else, games are no fun alone. It's no fun unless you can show it off."

So, when Bromley formed the Mayfair Games Company in 1981 to share and show off new games, Peter was named his vice president. But though the brothers were making games instead of just playing them, the way they felt about the games didn't change very much.

"We still hate to lose," Bromley said. "We're both very competitive. We are each other's worst critic. That's why we don't play each other as much as we used to. Losing to your brother has the same negative impact as always."

First as a player and later as a designer, Bromley watched different games rise in popularity. When he graduated from high school in 1968, military games were the rage.

"Back to 1960, war and strategy games dominated for fifteen years," Bromley said, "followed by fifteen years of role-playing games, followed by collectible card games. Each realm has reached a higher money level. In the 1970s, the fan swell for RPGs approached ten to fifteen million dollars. [After just two years,] CCGs were between one hundred and one hundred fifty million dollars."

Bromley believed that when *Magic: The Gathering* was introduced in 1993, the game-playing market was ready for a change. "Every product has a finite life cycle. Role-playing wasn't dead [in 1993], and it isn't still. But role-playing had run its life [in the forefront of] the marketplace."

Gamers were ready for a new challenge even sooner, but "in 1990 it was technically and financially impossible to create trading card games," Bromley said.

Printing by traditional methods meant that a single card cost hundreds of dollars in printing preparations—not even counting the cost of art or writing. A whole deck often cost tens of thousands of dollars before a single card was printed or sold.

But by 1993, desktop computer publishing had changed all that. Single cards soon cost less than $100 each to prepare for publication. Producers were ready to make collectible card games, and players were ready to buy them.

"*Magic* succeeded because the market was already in place, with shows, shops, and dealers," Bromley said. This was part of CCGs' quick success, but Bromley also saw that CCGs offered something new to players who had not received much attention before.

"Women make up twenty to thirty percent of gamers," Bromley said, observing that women gamers tend to like "high-level strategy games. They like games involving money, and games stressing language, like *Scrabble*." Women also tend not to play "traditional combat games," Bromley said.

But women do tend to like collectible card games. Based on market research, Bromley gave his idea why: "*Magic* suggests that no one dies, that magicians

MAYOR

Grants 2 votes. Breaks ties in council votes. Mayor must pay damages caused by disastrous events.

*Darwin Bromley, president and founder of Mayfair Games, doubles as the mayor of SimCity in his creation* SimCity The Card Game.

escape to a new plan when their life points are drained. That's more acceptable to women. Likewise, *Star Trek* has a more positive game goal of traversing the space continuum line and accomplishing missions, versus traditional combat."

Bromley's lifelong study of games allowed him to find other factors that helped CCGs become so popular so quickly. He compared *Magic* with another game, *Battle Cards*, both of which debuted during the same month in 1993.

*Battle Cards*, said Bromley, "were trading cards, and would crack when they were shuffled. You had to scratch off a portion of the card to reveal battle outcomes, so you had to either play the game or collect it. You couldn't have your cake and eat it, too." On the other hand, said Bromley, "*Magic* was sophisticated, a *playing* card. Yet collectors took to the slick nature of it."

Collectors value cards that are hard to find, or scarce. Players value cards because of their purpose in the game. Bromley pointed out two ways to judge the purpose of a collectible playing card.

"First, there's the customizable aspect. *Star Trek: The Next Generation* promotes this concept. This is terrifically beneficial," Bromley said, because customizing a deck is something a player can do alone. Playing an actual game usually requires another person. But, if it isn't possible to have a game, a player can still spend time alone building decks, shopping for special cards, practicing or reading up on new strategies. A card may have a special purpose in your particular, customized deck.

Another way to determine the purpose of a collectible playing card is to size up its raw power. Bromley pointed out that, in some CCGs, "rare cards make a huge difference." He called such powerful cards part of "the arms race."

"Younger players may see the arms race as the downside of collecting," Bromley said. "It's like in video games. Say my friend beats me. My friend has bought a new control stick. The game wasn't decided necessarily because my friend's a better player, but because he has better tools. So I have to buy the same thing to beat him better. The same holds true if my friend has a Black Lotus or Rock Hydra. That [card is] what beats me," Bromley said.

"Some games, like *Magic* and *Highlander*, encourage the arms race more. In these games, rare cards make a huge difference," he explained. "I avoided that when I designed *SimCity The Card Game*. In it, everyone draws from one common deck, even though you can still customize the game. It's the only satisfying solitaire game so far."

## Secrets for Success

Knowing what makes a game popular is a crucial part of game design. That's why collecting games, originally a hobby for Darwin Bromley, is now an important part of his work as a game designer.

"I'd say the same thing to anyone who wanted to be a writer, work in film, or do anything creative—learn as much as you can about everything that has been done. Do it critically. Peter and I have collected over six thousand games," Bromley said.

Believe it or not, researching games may be a tough job. Bromley believes that the only way to research and learn about games is to put together your own library of games, just like Thomas Jefferson and Benjamin Franklin put together their own libraries of books.

"You don't have to do all games. Concentrate on two hundred to three hundred," he advised. "And, you don't have to be a good game player." Bromley believes that game designers are often handicapped by what they want a card game to do—as opposed to what the game actually does.

*Darwin Bromley analyzed the success and strategy of many games in the process of designing* SimCity The Card Game.

"If I see an incongruous element in a game, I want to fix it," Bromley said. "Other players may think, 'How can using that oddity in the game help me win?' [They've] analyzed the game in ways I couldn't."

An important part of game design is knowing your own strengths. "I've tended to follow the path of my own abilities," Bromley said. "I worked six years as a tax attorney, and am still a licensed attorney. My work in law has been with wills, trusts, and taxes. I'm trained to write rules, rules that can be enforceable by courts." Of course, this has helped Bromley write clear, fair rules for games.

Yet his first collegiate degree was in math. Game designers, Bromley said, "have to understand the principles of math. Statistics is the number one curriculum. To make a game, you need to know frequency distribution and possible outcomes from dice."

But game designers also need "facility with language. The gaming industry is a worldwide market. For example, I'm going to an Essen Games Convention in Germany. The three years of German I took in college will serve me well," he said. In the first decade of the twenty-first century, when there will be an even greater international exchange, he added, "game designers will need an even greater facility with language."

Bromley believes that games are more than entertainment.

"What do kids get out of CCGs?" he asked. "The same skills they get from playing RPGs, plus organizational talents, strategies for handling money, and a casual self-respect. In bargaining and dealing for cards, kids are learning a skill that will carry over to other parts of life. When they aren't paying book values for their cards, that means they'll be able to go through life negotiating and making deals for cars, or even corporations."

For Bromley, business is a game within a game. "I'm still a capitalist," he smiled. "I have to raise money to buy games."

# *Chapter*

## 5

# THE MAKING OF GRIDIRON

Collectible card games started as a gaming cloudburst, and quickly turned into a flash flood. Before the game genre was two years old, store shelves were crowded with new products. Game companies knew that every collectible card game had to be a new and improved idea to succeed. So how does a good game get dreamed up?

Often, the answer lies in taking bits and pieces from many worlds, as the doctors Frankenstein and Garfield did.

Early CCG makers couldn't figure out how to hook collectors of sports cards. These collectors seemed like logical buyers—after all, they already knew the ins and outs of card collecting. But the closest that sports fans had come to gaming was "fantasy football," a way of using current players and their statistics to create made-up teams and games on paper.

Arizona-based Precedence Publishing noted these facts while dreaming up a CCG called *GridIron Fantasy Football*. The twenty-employee company started in 1984, first gaining notice for making the role-playing game *Immortal*.

Paul Brown, Precedence spokesman and game producer, said, "*GridIron* is football of the future. It has elements of the movies *Rollerball* and *The Longest Yard*." This football game has the same adventure and action found in games like *Ultimate Combat!* and *Overpower*. That's why the cards provide for trash-talking insults, terrorists hijacking the scoreboard to change the results, and other surprises.

Of course, Precedence didn't make the game happen alone. They joined forces with Upper Deck. After printing *Rage*, a success created by White Wolf, Upper Deck had firsthand knowledge of the popularity of

CCGs. That's why Upper Deck executives showed up at the 1995 Game Manufacturers Association (GAMA) trade show in New Orleans, scouting out a way to get more involved. When Precedence announced their plan for *GridIron* to the attendees, Upper Deck wanted to participate.

Before Upper Deck would help with *GridIron*, the company insisted on play-testing with various age groups and conducting other market research.

"Play-testing for young players is a lot like the story from *Charley and the Chocolate Factory*," producer Brown said. "It seems like fun, but there's an element of work to it. You're not using the final cards with the sophisticated graphics yet, or rules in their finished forms. A lot of younger play-testers don't pan out."

## Getting It Right

One of the first decisions was how the cards should look. Conceptual artist Kelly Godine created more than 100 cards. "We used over 40 artists to create *GridIron*," Brown said. "CCGs have become a significant venue for fantasy artists."

*Some say* GridIron Fantasy Football *is the "football of the future." This new collectible card game from Precedence Publishing and Upper Deck requires the same strategies as the real-world game of football—plus the flexibility to handle out-of-this-world surprises.*

More than 300 cards were in the first set. A starter deck contained 60 cards, a rule book, a score sheet, and instructions on how to form a league. This design went beyond how one game would be played.

The sports theme was stretched to encourage gamers to keep playing *GridIron* every week, setting a schedule to keep win-loss standings and actually complete a full fantasy season. Upper Deck kept collectors in mind by inserting special "chase" cards in only a few packs. (An average of 1 of every 23 packs would contain a high-powered insert card, which required collectors to "chase" after the cards.)

Precedence was challenged by creating a new type of CCG. Upper Deck, though a respected and experienced collectible sports-card maker, found itself faced with a new challenge, too: selling to an audience that wasn't aware of gaming cards. A game needs players, whether the game is football on the field or football on playing cards.

To find players, the companies had to decide what they were looking for. Although all kinds of people play games, Upper Deck decided that *GridIron* would most likely appeal to males, ages twelve to thirty. Company literature named these players as the game's target audience, those most likely to play—and keep playing—the game. The company sent out fact sheets to sports-card dealers, trying to persuade them to sell the new game in their stores.

Upper Deck's original promotional literature estimated the CCG market at $250 to $500 million for 1994, with fifty percent growth expected for 1995. They pointed out that circulation of CCG magazines exceeded 800,000.

The team of Precedence designers included Dave Hewitt, who laughingly calls himself a "legate" (pronounced LEG-it). "That's the title we grant to certain people here at Precedence," he says, "meaning someone who's authorized to speak with the voice of the Emperor."

Hewitt remembered the beginnings of *GridIron*. "We had created *Slasher* previously, a CCG that taught us what it takes to make a good card game. It was a learning experience for us," he says. After that, discussions about developing a football game began.

"Back in February 1995, we decided we'd go ahead. We did a complete reversal on *GridIron* in March. There was a drastic revision. The original was a good simulation of football, using cards. It felt very much like football. But it wasn't fun. It was a time-consuming, stat-based comparison at first. We wanted more back-and-forth interaction."

Hewitt brought special skills to designing *GridIron*, admitting, "I am the biggest football fan in the company. I'm the only one who reads the sports pages every day. But everyone at Precedence has played games for years. We had played *Magic*, but stopped. We all still play *Jyhad* and *Shadowfist*. And *GridIron*, of course!"

Having fun playing games can be good homework. "It helps a lot," Hewitt said. "Anyone can take the basic pieces of a game and slap them together. However, it requires gaming experience to learn what not to put in. It's like putting a jigsaw puzzle together. There's a temptation to put everything in. You learn when to say no.

"I started playing *Dungeons & Dragons* at age six or seven, when my father brought it home. We all played. Also, we played card games like *War*, and video games."

Hewitt's childhood game-playing allowed him to make *GridIron* more kid-friendly. "Kids are smart. They'll pick up a game. I know I have no time to read a sixty- to eighty-page rule book. There's a lot you can pick up as you go along in *GridIron*," he said.

"Like *Nintendo*, we wanted a Quick Start Guide. Then, after more games, you could come back to the rule book to learn more. For the introductory level rules, I say, let 'em play, and stay at that rate if they're happy," Hewitt added.

Hewitt and the *GridIron* design team resisted the temptation to rely on game-stopping killer cards. "Some cards are mathematically better. But we wanted to include counters, so there's always a way to beat a card," he said. "If some cards or combinations of cards seem impossible to challenge, then we'll pull a card from a set. The more freedom a player has [in playing cards] the happier he is. The more flexibility a player has, the more fun he has."

Hewitt predicted that different *Grid-Iron* playing styles wouldn't be limited to a gamer's age. "If you know football, you can apply sports strategy to *GridIron*, using intuitive knowledge. A gamer can have different insights, making different card-play combinations. Or, the third level of play means simply turning your mind off and playing the symbols."

Despite *GridIron*'s gritty and combative theme, Hewitt himself spoke as if he simply loves the teamwork that almost any game can provide—including the ever-growing number of CCGs. "I welcome others," Hewitt said. "I'm always looking for a good game to play."

# *Chapter*

# 6

# THE COLLECTING GAME

Part of the fun of collectible card games is customizing your deck. Depending on the game, the deck you play with may include forty cards or more, but you must choose those few from hundreds of possibilities.

You can buy collectible cards at game and hobby shops, comics and sports-card shops, even at some bookstores, department and grocery stores. The cards are sold in a variety of pack sizes.

"Starter decks" usually number about sixty cards for games that need from forty to sixty cards per player. Be careful when buying a new game: Not all companies guarantee that a starter deck will contain the right combination of cards to play. If the package does not clearly state that the contents are "ready to play," ask a clerk or check a hobby magazine for more information.

"Booster packs" usually contain from eight to fifteen cards. These packs cost more per card than the starter decks, but may promise a certain number of "uncommon" cards that your opponents aren't likely to have.

"Uncommon," "rare," and "ultra-rare" are hobby terms describing the scarcity of a card. The words mean that the game publisher does not print as many of this type of card as it prints of "common" cards. Because fewer rare cards exist, you'll have more trouble finding one in a starter or booster pack. Precise numbers of rare cards printed vary from publisher to publisher, but some game companies reveal these numbers in hobby magazines.

For instance, the Decipher company told hobby magazines that the first release of *Star Trek: The Next Generation* contained 363 cards. The set was divided into thirds: 121 common cards, 121 uncommon, and 121 rare. The print run of the Limited Edition totaled 45,900,000 cards, breaking down to 281,157 of each common, 78,843 of each uncommon, and 19,339 of each rare. For fans of ratios, you'll guess that more than three times as many commons were printed as uncommons. In addition, commons outnumbered rare cards fourteen to one.

## Inside Views

Magazines focusing on collectible card games began to appear just one year after *Magic: The Gathering* debuted. The first was *Scrye* (which rhymes with "sky"), a combination magazine and price guide.

Price guides give card customers an idea of fair prices for specific cards and sets. According to Joanne White, *Scrye's* first editor, "Single cards from customizable card games become valuable based on how they affect a game." Rare cards of *Magic: The Gathering* sold singly for widely varying prices two years after release, she said. The same number had been printed of each rare

Scrye *was the first magazine devoted to collectible card games, with prices and checklists, game reviews, articles, and ads. Originally designed for shop owners, gamers of all ages quickly adopted this magazine, leading other companies to start similar publications.*

71

card, yet most sold for fifteen dollars or less, while the card called the Black Lotus brought ten times that amount. "The Lotus is as rare as the other cards, but it does something different in the game," White said.

The Black Lotus was so different that opponents often couldn't figure out a way to fight it. Later, Wizards stopped making the card, in order to keep the game fun.

Often, fewer of the cards with unusual powers are printed. After all, how exciting would baseball be if every batter hit a home run? Some of the most suspenseful games are won with only single hits, walks, stolen bases, bunts, slides, and other "common" plays.

This is why truly devoted card players value inexpensive cards, too. Used properly, decks of low-powered cards can beat hands with Black Lotuses and other powerful cards. Jokingly called "weenie" decks because they look insignificant, such sets succeed because attack cards need fewer "helper" cards to start causing damage.

White stressed that cards are collectible beyond their playability "because many people want complete sets." Scarcity doesn't always mean a card is worth more in a game, although scarcity always means a card is worth more money.

"This new game genre of collectible, customizable card games has created the combination collector/player," White said.

## Collector/Players

The term "collector/player" explains how collectors of trading card games differ from other card collectors. Most card collectors simply look at their possessions. Card-game collectors play with theirs.

When people only look at their collectibles, looks become very important. Many baseball-card and other memorabilia collectors demand that items in their collections look like new. A little scratch can alter the value of some treasures by half, because replacing these rare items is difficult.

Condition is important to the value of collectible cards for a much more practical reason: If a playing card is too worn out, that card could be considered "marked." Marked cards are illegal to play with. If some cards are marked, you can easily identify them and see when you will draw them into your hand. With this advantage, you can plan your strategy farther ahead than your opponent, which is not fair.

To keep cards in good playing condition longer, collector/players often have one set of cards to play with and one to store away. But what happens when months or years of use wears out the playing set? To avoid this dilemma, many players place each card in an individual plastic sleeve which can be purchased at hobby/game shops or ordered from sources in hobby magazines. Players who use some types of protective sleeves have found that game set-up takes longer because it's awkward to shuffle cards that are in plastic.

## Mint, Fine, Very Fine, Poor

For years, hobbyists of many sorts have used condition guidelines to help them buy, sell, and trade items. The terms used to describe the condition of collectible gaming cards are borrowed from collectible sports cards. However, only the words are borrowed. The meanings are quite different with gaming cards, allowing much more game-related wear.

*Mint:* A card classified as Mint looks, and is, brand new and unused.

A near-mint card, like the one pictured here, is basically brand new. The corners still have curved, factory-cut shapes, with no uneven wear. The card is shiny and unscuffed. Price guides usually list what to pay for cards in near-mint conditon.

*Near Mint:* You'll find flaws in a Near Mint card only with careful scrutiny. Hairline scratches are allowed on the card backs and "up to three" slight marks on the cards' edges, according to *Scrye* magazine.

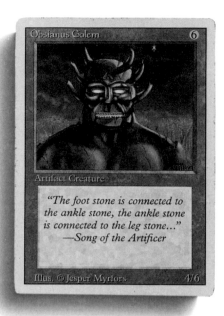

*A fine card has seen some game action. Every edge shows a little wear. The die-cut corners are worn down. Some fine-line dents show. These are acceptable for play.*

*Very Fine:* A Very Fine card has light scratches and wear marks on the edges. Its primary flaw is simply age and the loss of gloss that comes with it.

*Fine:* A card graded Fine has one or two white, worn edges that show on one side when the card is laid flat. Scratches are not visible enough to mark the card for play. Investor/collectors often do not include cards rated Fine or lower in their sets, although player/collectors do.

*Very Good:* A card with this rating shows white on both sides of the card. A few scratches, even almost-invisible creases, are allowed in this category. These cards are legal in play, as long as they are not easily identifiable when they are with the other cards in the deck.

*Good:* Good cards show more wear than just creases, worn edges, and scratches; they show the wear that comes from being held and rubbed by fingers countless times. They are still acceptable for play if they are not easily identifiable, but with dirt marks and up to four white edges, Good cards are often considered marked.

*Fair:* Any card that has been written on by an owner is automatically classified as Fair. Even so, some players—including Richard Garfield, creator of *Magic: The Gathering*—have the losing player initial cards lost in an ante game. These initialed cards provide a history of the people who have owned them, all of whom have been

*A good card has the same troubles a fine card has, only bigger. White hairline scratches are visible. Cards in good condition are acceptable for play as long as no marks distinguish them from the rest of the deck.*

symbolically beaten by the new owner. But history is not Mint. Writing aside, Fair cards have severe wear and crease marks, with all four edges white and worn.

*Poor:* A Poor card is a bent, marked, worn-bald, dirty mess. Parts of a Poor card may

Conservator 4

Mono Artifact

**3**: Prevent the
loss of up to 2 life.

Illus. © Amy Weber

*Poor cards have lost their shininess. Wear is found all over the card, not just at the edges, with bends and scratches, even pen or pencil marks. They are not allowed in tournament play.*

be missing. It's unacceptable for play, and only acceptable to a collector who just wants to complete a set.

These classifications make it clear that collectible card games appeal to two groups: players and collectors. Emphasis on collecting or playing varies from person to person, and even from game to game.

For example, some collectible card games, such as *Magic: The Gathering*, feature cards that are collectible because of their power in a game. Other games, like *Star Trek: The Next Generation*, have cards of fairly similar strengths. Here, the collectibility of the cards may be based on other factors, such as the popularity of a certain television character pictured on the card.

These different reasons for collecting can even affect card values. For example, any writing on an otherwise perfect card should decrease that card's classification to Fair. Yet, fans of the *Star Trek* television show might consider a card more valuable if autographed by the pictured actor.

## Autographed Cards

The question "To autograph, or not to autograph?" has been asked among baseball-card collectors, comic-book collectors, and other print collectors for years. The answer is still a matter of opinion.

Some collectors approve of autographs by a game's creator (such as *SuperDeck!*'s Marc Miller) or the artist whose work is reprinted on the card (such as *SuperDeck!*'s comic-book artist Danny Adkins, known for his work with *Superman*). Likewise, in sports-card collecting, some people believe a card is more valuable if the pictured athlete signs it. These collectors see an autograph as a unique feature of the card and feel that if an autograph doesn't raise a card's value, it surely can't hurt it.

Gaming-card collectors may be able to come up with an answer, due to two unique differences between sports cards and gaming cards.

The first difference began when *Magic: The Gathering* set a standard for the collectible-card-game industry by boldly printing artists' names on the cards the artists designed. Collectors can easily identify an artist by style and name. Lots of art styles are used so that every player can find something to like and then look for other work by favorite artists.

More important for collectors, however, is another industry standard set by Wizards of the Coast. The company clearly marks reprinted *Magic: The Gathering* cards with new border colors or special inset symbols. This way, collectors can be sure that rare *Magic* cards are truly rare.

If you *admire a certain artist or game
designer, you might want to have a
favorite card autographed by its creator.
Because some other collectors think sig-
natures are graffiti, it's best not to have a
card autographed unless you plan never
to trade it.*

The more expensive original will have a
different symbol than later editions of the
same card. An autograph collector might
especially enjoy signed versions of the oldest, rarest cards.

## Promo Cards

Short for "promotional cards," promo cards are the "wild cards" in many otherwise limited sets. Promo cards are given away at conventions (gatherings of gamers and game manufacturers) or in special issues of hobby magazines. Some promo cards must be obtained through mail-in offers.

Promo cards may be reprints of cards from the regular set. If so, these are always common cards, nice to add in to play, but bound not to be worth much money. On the other hand, promo cards are sometimes created especially for an event, occasion, or publication. Are these promos automatically rare?

Maybe, maybe not.

Just because a card's production was limited at first doesn't mean it will be limited forever. Even if the card was never sold in starter or booster packs, that's no guarantee that the card will be scarce. Perhaps the company has given the card free to everyone attending comic-book, gaming-

Promotional, or promo, cards are given as bonuses for buying certain products, or given as samples at game shops and conventions. Promos may be included in magazines that relate to collectible card games, such as this SimCity promo included in an issue of COMBO magazine. Since SimCity is a game about building an urban area, the COMBO offices were pictured on the promo card.

card, or sports-card conventions for months. And if the card is not attractive or particularly useful in play, only "one-of-everything collectors," not active gamers, would want it. Only time will tell if a particular promo is rare.

Promo cards would not be included in factory sets. Factory-collated card sets first appeared in sports cards in the 1980s. This collector option soon appeared for a few CCGs.

If a CCG company releases a "complete set," this probably won't include expansion sets. Those subsets may or may not be released in their own complete factory sets later.

Collectible card games were created just after baseball cards went through a cycle of fame and collecting them became a prosperous business. That's why some gamers caught investment fever, too. But the baseball-card market also hit a decline after its success, and investor/collectors lost money.

The best advice for player/collectors is advice that has been given to baseball-card collectors for years: Collect what you enjoy. Don't buy into the idea of investing for the future. The point of a hobby is to have fun now.

# *Chapter*

# 7

# GAMES IN THE 'HOOD

A hobby belongs to anyone who loves it. That's why the best hobby shops belong to two kinds of people—those who work in the shops for a living, and those who care about what the shops provide.

Rob Josephson is both. He grew up reading the same comic books he now sells in his own shop, Mayhem Comics and Collectibles in Ames, Iowa. At first, Mayhem was a small sports-card and comics shop, and Josephson worked for somebody else.

In 1989 he bought the business, but he hasn't stopped learning about it.

"Word of mouth is the best way to learn in this business," he said. For example, in 1993, a customer told Josephson about seeing a new card game at a convention. So Josephson ordered a few boxes of *Magic: The Gathering*. The cards sold slowly at first. "I can't believe now that it took so long for those to sell," said Josephson.

"Customers taught us all about the game. They had read about it in magazines." And they helped Josephson and his partners learn to play. "When you have peers to teach you, you can pick up the game really quickly.

"Just from the period between fall, when we first got it, and Christmas, we could see that this was going to be really big," he said.

Two years later, Josephson said that the game was "still a fad. But it's also becoming an integral part of the gaming industry. We've got two-hundred-dollar cards now, and maybe that part of it is a fad. But I think the game itself has found a niche in the industry."

Other collectible card games have crowded into that niche—so many, in fact, that choosing a new game to learn is sometimes more difficult than actually learning the game.

Josephson suggests that newcomers to CCGs go into a shop and "walk toward the crowd. If there's a crowd around a new game, the game must be good."

Next, he said, ask how available the game is. Can you get starter decks and boosters?

A starter deck and a booster pack are the only investments that Josephson advises for beginners. "Always start out small," he said. But, before making any purchase, look for an opportunity to watch experienced players in action. "Sit in on a game. Instructions books are good, but experiencing the game is better. If you don't like the game, then you haven't lost much," Josephson said. "I always tell a kid, look for something you think looks neat."

Ask if a game costs a lot of money to get into. In the early years of CCGs, a $10 to $15 start-up cost was "pretty good," Josephson said. "But remember that a seller may not always be entirely truthful. If a game is boring, a shop owner might over-sell it," trying to convince shoppers that the game is popular or just about to hit it big. "If a game is selling well, then the

Cards in many
games rise or fall in
value according to the
power the cards have in play.
But singles from the game based
upon the TV series Star Trek: The Next
Generation *are considered more collectible
when a popular character is featured.*

owner will just tell you about it" without the hard sell, Josephson added.

Finally, Josephson's advice is, "Ask a person who knows the game to explain it. I can tell when people talk like they really love a game. They want to sit down and explain it. The way a person explains can tell you a lot," he said.

Once you've selected a game you'd like to try, don't let your hobby cost too much. "I always say, don't spend a nickel in my store until you know what you want to buy," Josephson said. He adds a warning that young players shouldn't get involved with games that can become too expensive.

"*Magic* is an expensive game, if you allow it to be," he said. But "you can win with regular cards. Wizards of the Coast is bringing back reprints of early cards, so people can play" without spending lots of money buying the original rare cards.

Even packages can be cheaper, depending on where you buy. Josephson recommends that card buyers look for the suggested retail price, the price printed on the packaging by the manufacturer. Some retailers mark popular games with higher prices, to make extra profit. If this is happening at the store you go to, ask other gamers where they shop.

# Trading

For Josephson's store, Mayhem, individual card sales is "where the money is." Collectors bring in cards (or comics, or other items Josephson sells) that they'd like to sell or trade for something else.

"We had to establish a universal buy-back policy even before there were collectible card games," Josephson said, "and that is usually fifty percent. We pay a customer selling back his comics fifty percent of what the price guide says those comics are worth."

Why only half? Because Josephson wants to sell the used items to somebody else. And somebody else may not want to pay Josephson more than the price-guide price. But that possible 50 percent profit isn't always money in the bank for the shop owner.

"Everything in this store has to be paid for," Josephson explained. "Electricity, lights, rent, plumbing, us, all the new merchandise"—all the expenses of running a business, which are called overhead, quickly lessen profits.

"We want to be fair," Josephson said, "because if we turn a customer off to one hobby, we might turn him off to all hobbies. But we also have to look at (buying or trading) as a business deal" in order to make money to keep the store running.

Because many shop owners like Josephson use price guides to regulate costs, choosing a price guide is an important business decision. Different price guides may have different ideas about card values. Which price guide to choose is a matter of opinion, but choosing one is important, so buyers and sellers know what to expect.

"We look for a price guide that takes prices from a conglomeration of stores and then figures the average," Josephson said.

Although Josephson pays 50 percent of "book" (the price-guide listing) for comics resold in his shop, he buys back CCG cards at 40 percent of the median price in his preferred price guide.

"That's because, with these cards, what's hot here is not always what's hot somewhere else in the country," he explained. "But CCG prices do remain pretty constant, much more so than comics prices. With our prices the way they are, we won't get shoved out of the market by high-end buyers [store owners who can afford to buy mass quantities of cards at a discount, then sell at less of a profit]. But we won't have someone come off the street and buy all of our cards because we're too cheap, either.

"If you're looking for a better price, then you need to sell on your own" directly to another player, Josephson said. "But then you might be taken advantage of. Kids here know what they're getting."

Like many shop owners, Josephson goes a little higher—up to 50 percent—on trades. But "we found out very quickly not to trade *Magic*, because that's all we'd do," he said. "We'll still trade *Magic* once in awhile, but we want to do a lot in one swap," such as a whole collection.

Some customers ask for a discount when they buy a lot of product, and many retailers agree. Josephson reported that "a lot of people want discounts on boxes of *Magic*. But because *Magic* is such a terrific product, we don't need to [discount it]. People can get discounts through the mail, but they can also be ripped off through mail-order services or the product can be damaged in transit. We don't overcharge on the product, but we want some padding to make up for the experiments and for other extras."

## Sharing the Adventure

"Experiments" are new games that both Josephson and his customers know little about. After all, judging a game's fun factor is tough if you've never actually played.

"If someone wants to try a new game, we'll order one box and see how it goes," Josephson said. Mayhem learned that system the hard way: When a reputable game company came out with its first CCG, Mayhem "bought a lot, but wound up giving it away." Even though giving cards away meant losing some money, moving the unpopular cards meant room on store shelves to sell something else. Losses like this are why Josephson doesn't discount popular games.

But he still experiments. In fact, "We do more experimentation now, sometimes buying only one box of a new game to start. If we sell half, the box is paid for." And the customers know that their store is willing to provide them with the games that they want to play, rather than expecting them to choose from just the games already in stock.

Federation

STAR TREK
THE NEXT GENERATION

Earth is a member of the United Federation of Planets. The
Federation establishes outposts throughout its territory.

Seed one if playing Federation OR build later at any
location where a Federation ENGINEER is present.

SHIELDS 30

OUTPOST

Federation

STAR TREK
THE NEXT GENERATION

Earth is a member of the United Federation of Planets. The
Federation establishes outposts throughout its territory.

Seed one if playing Federation OR build later at any
location where a Federation ENGINEER is present.

SHIELDS 30

OUTPOST

Limited edition cards, like
this black-bordered Star Trek card, are printed
in set quantities, making these cards more rare
and thus worth more money. Unlimited edition
cards, like the white-bordered card, are printed
in huge quantities. Edition type makes a difference on prices, but the cards play the same,
limited or not.

Josephson recalled advertising a *Magic* tournament at Mayhem only to discover, "We couldn't get the revised cards required for tournament play. The only way we could get them was at retail, and we sold them at retail and took a loss because we wanted to have that tournament for our customers. We paid for people knowing we'd go that extra mile for them. It let our customers know that the shop belongs to them, as well as to us. We wanted to bring back the mom-and-pop neighborhood feeling. If customers get both fun and service, that's the best promotion we can do. And we have fun, too. We're here to make a living, but also to enjoy."

Josephson and his fun-loving Mayhem partners converted the basement of their store into a game room. Anyone is welcome, no time limit or purchase requirements. Newcomers may see the space as a wildlife refuge for gamers, and puzzle over why the owners didn't make it into more sales space.

"The players are going to be here for twenty years. Players are the life-blood and soul of the game," Josephson said. "People who want to make a buck—it's their choice. But it's neat to see people who really love the game. I love to sell to people who really cherish the cards."

# *Chapter*

## 8

# HOW TO WIN FRIENDS AND INFLUENCE PEOPLE

One of the best things about games is that you need other people to play with. You can joke together, eat together, argue together (in a friendly way, of course), and that's all part of the fun.

One of the worst things about games is that you need other people to play with.

You've got to convince your family or friends that this strange-sounding activity is fun, that you won't abandon other activities you've shared in the past, that you won't think people are foolish if they don't get all the rules right away.

A lot of games—especially collectible card games—make use of diplomatic skills: persuading people, working as a team, negotiating trades. Using these skills to find other players gives you valuable practice even before the game begins.

## Finding People to Play

You may find new, enthusiastic players among people you already know. Friends are ideal first students: While you teach them the game, they'll teach you how to teach simply by being your students and letting you practice your skills.

If you find that your friends enjoy other activities more, you can add new game companions to your circle of friends. Post notices at school, in local hobby and comics shops, and at the public library. State that you are looking for players for a collectible card game and would like to start a group. The group may wind up having only two members, or you may get six or more. You may get an even better response if you make it clear that you'll be glad to teach newcomers how to play.

To drum up more interest, you could write a short article for your school newspaper. But remember to write about the most important thing: what makes your favorite game fun. No matter how important it may seem to explain each and every rule, remember that most new players want to hear about the fun first. (Didn't you?)

Don't forget that some quality opponents may live at your house or be related to you. You may feel awkward teaching complicated new games to your parents, grandparents, or other adults. After all, grown-ups have always taught you. Chances are, this discomfort doesn't really have much to do with age—it has to do with learning to teach. Even grown-ups can feel funny teaching other grown-ups at first. But once you are convinced that your student wants to learn, and that you can teach what you know, age shouldn't matter. "The play is the thing," as Shakespeare said.

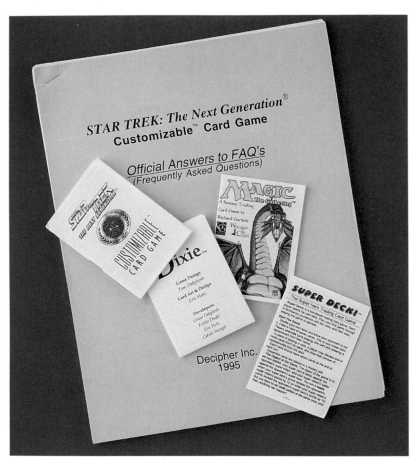

Many CCG players like the fact that there's always more to learn about a favorite game. Start-up instruction books range from eight pages (SuperDeck!) to forty-seven pages (Magic). Enthusiastic players often come up with more questions during actual games. That's why many companies print answers to frequently asked questions (FAQs), like the packet seen here from Star Trek: The Next Generation.

## Teaching People to Play

Teaching is a tough business. Students can't really have much fun until they learn the rules. For example, students want to jump on their bicycles and ride to great places; their teachers try to persuade them to learn traffic rules first.

Remind your students (and yourself!) that games are supposed to be fun. In fact, use the word "game" as often as you can when you're teaching. Instead of telling new players "the rules" (which sounds serious), tell them "how the game works" (which sounds more like fun).

Decide which rules are the most important and concentrate on teaching those first. Decide which five facts players need to know in order to actually play. First things first: What good is teaching people how to tie their shoes if they keep putting them on the wrong feet? Take your students step by step and don't worry if only one step is learned. One step is a start! And an inspiration—a person who can get those shoes on the right feet is going to really want to learn to tie them.

Learning is more fun if the knowledge can be used, practiced, and proven. That's when all those rules make sense—and even become part of the fun.

Let your student practice two or three rules at a time. Select cards for a beginner's deck that have easy-to-understand commands, cards that can do something without needing lots of other cards to help. As your pupil watches you construct a beginner's deck, tell how you included so many of this kind of card and not very many of that. If your student asks why, your answer should be, "Let's play and find out!"

Start playing as quickly as you can. During the game, give your student problems that are easy to solve. Everyone loves to be successful. Succeeding makes a person want to succeed again and curious about how to accomplish it. When the first rules have been mastered, choose the next most important rules and help your student practice them.

Eager students are so much fun to teach, you might be tempted to jump ahead and teach lots of complex rules at once. If your student really is catching on, go ahead. But pay close attention: If your student gets tired or grumpy, that's probably a sign you need to slow down. Make sure your student feels confident and really understands what you've covered before you go on to new information.

Some teachers try to ensure their students' success by losing on purpose, cheating in reverse. That might boost confidence for a moment, but it also might ultimately sour the new player on the game. Why should anyone go on playing if it's so easy? The fun in games is conquering a challenge, having something impressive to talk to your friends about.

On the other hand, new players who only know a few rules aren't going to appreciate you or the game if you play too hard too soon. Defeat after defeat could easily discourage new players. That could cheat you out of a teacher's best reward: a worthy opponent, eager to share the game.

## Tips and Tools for Teaching

Even though many collectible card games are designed to be played by two players with two decks, it's possible to share one deck and have a good game, so that new

+7

**Anti-Tank Missile**

Also removes any land Vehicle used by opponent.

An anti-tank missile must carry enough power to punch through a foot or more of high-grade steel. It will also punch through cars and trucks.

**Plus**

Copyright © 1994 CSI.
Illo © Vince Musacchia.

-7

**Falling Airliner**

Struck by an experimental anti-aircraft missile, and now plunging to its doom unless someone can save it!

**Minus**

**H**

Copyright © 1994 CSI.
Illo © Dan Davis.

*Prepare your deck to add points to your score, subtract points from your opponent's, and protect yourself from damage that your opponent attempts against you. These SuperDeck! cards illustrate the idea.*

players can learn without wasting money on games they may not like.

Here are some ways to get started teaching and playing. Decide which suggestions work best with your game.

- *Play early matches "open hand" to make it easy to explain rules in action.* Both players lay their hands of cards face up on the table. You can explain to your student why and how you are making your plays ("You forgot to protect your territory like we talked about, so now I'm going to attack!").

- *Play with two players, one hand, one large deck, and one discard pile.* Deal the hand face up on the table. During your turn, the hand is yours; you draw cards into the hand and take cards from the hand into your territory. When it is your student's turn, he draws into the hand and takes cards for his territory. This can lead to some very tricky strategy. Should you take a card that you don't really need because your opponent could use it against you?

- *Play with two players, two hands of cards, one deck, and one discard pile.* To play this way, you need to join two decks of cards into one big deck, so that the game will have time to unfold. (You may have enough extras to form the extra deck, or you could borrow the deck from another player you know.) Be sure to select cards of fairly equal powers, so the game will depend on some playing skill instead of who draws the killer card.

- *If you have extra cards, or enough to make two decks, lend or give your friend some of your cards.* It doesn't matter if neither deck is very strong. You don't want anybody to be unbeatable, anyway— part of the fun is the challenge. Teaching a new player how to put a deck together will make her feel like an expert, too.

When your students begin adding their own thoughts and ideas, they will be able to teach you even more about the game you love. You'll know you are a successful teacher when you start learning from your students.

## When Is a Hobby Not a Hobby Anymore?

A hobby can be like a friend: No matter how long you've known each other, there are still surprises and new discoveries to make about each other. But learning about friends is almost always free. Spending time with a hobby often means spending money.

Learning about money and time management is an added bonus of a hobby. Lily Garfield, Educational Games Coordinator at Wizards of the Coast, learned this as a student at the University of Pennsylvania. The challenges of gaming helped members of a games group there manage their free time more responsibly. According to Garfield, many members spent less time "partying" after the group formed.

But hobbies can sometimes turn into bad habits, too, particularly if they become too important in a person's life. While Garfield and her friends were gaming responsibly, others at the college had to delay graduation a semester or more because they skipped too many classes in order to play games.

How do you know if you're spending too much time on a hobby? Here are some questions that may help you answer that question regarding collectible card games. Answer honestly and check all the answers that apply to you.

1. Have you ever been so involved with a game that you:
   ____ missed a meal?
   ____ stayed up all night?
   ____ canceled plans with family or friends?

2. In school, do you:
   ____ have trouble concentrating because you are planning or anticipating a game?
   ____ get lower grades than you did before you started gaming?

3. Since you began gaming, do you think your friends:
   ____ don't like you as much as before?
   ____ only like you because you all play the same games?

4. To keep your family from worrying, have you ever:
   ____ lied about how much time you spend playing?

_____ lied about how much money you spend playing?

_____ asked for an advance on your allowance in order to buy cards?

_____ taken money for cards from a family member without asking permission?

5. After playing, do you feel:

_____ better about yourself if you've won?

_____ worse about yourself if you've lost?

_____ that losing means you ought to play again and try to win?

_____ that winning means you ought to play again and win some more?

6. When deciding how to spend free time, have you:

_____ tried to cut down on playing time, but failed?

_____ felt restless and irritable if you didn't make time to play?

_____ planned a game because you were upset about something else?

_____ given up other activities you enjoy because there wasn't enough time to do those things and play games?

If you made any checks in the first three sections, think of some new ways to manage your time. After all, gaming is supposed to be fun with friends, not something that stops you from having fun with friends. Start setting time limits on your games—even if you have to leave a game unfinished—so you have time to enjoy and learn from "non-game" activities and friends. Your brain needs a balanced diet just like your body does. You'll probably find that games are more fun if you have a variety of other activities in your life.

If you made any checks in the last three sections, you're taking your hobby pretty seriously. But completing this questionnaire proves you're able to look at yourself objectively. That's the beginning of balance. Talk to a trustworthy adult about your quiz results if you're concerned.

Helpful adults can be found by telephone, too. One resource is Nine-Line (1-800-999-9999), a toll-free service available 24 hours a day, with counseling referrals and support for teens and parents.

# Chapter

## 9

# WAYS TO PLAY

Everyone was a new player once. Experienced players may not know if they'll be able to beat a newcomer. But they can probably predict the mistakes beginners are about to make; they probably made those same mistakes, too, once upon a time.

Before joining the games table at the hobby shop or challenging players at school, ask yourself if you are falling into any of these common traps:

## The World's Biggest Deck

In many games, there is no limit to the number of cards you can use in a deck. Players who can't decide on a strategy often think there's strength in numbers. This kind of player often uses every card she owns in a game and tries to improve by getting more cards.

Too many cards actually weaken your game. Your most powerful cards may not be drawn during most of the game because they're trapped under less useful cards. Mathematicians call the chance that a certain card will be drawn at a certain time "probability." If there are lots of cards in the deck, there is less probability that you will draw the one you want.

## An Unbalanced Deck

Having an unbalanced deck doesn't mean you're a messy shuffler! Decks become unbalanced if a player follows one plan too closely. If you stack your deck to attack your opponent at every turn, you may be short on

*Buying boosters is a gamble. Though special cards are included, you won't know which ones until you have paid. But that's part of the game, whether you're a collector completing a set or a gamer studying strategies.*

cards to defend against surprises. Likewise, a deck arranged only to counter a foe's advances won't score many points quickly.

## The Confused Collector

It's easy to buy a price-guide magazine to find out which cards are rare, and almost as easy to pay big bucks to get them. Some beginners think having these cards will guarantee victory. It's risky to rely on only one or two cards. There's no promise that the right card will be drawn at the right time. And no card can guarantee victory if it's not played properly. If you're tempted to get a certain "power" card, even though you can't afford it, think twice. How would you play that card? How could another player beat it? Could combining cards produce as much power?

## The "Me Too!" Player

It's good to learn from every game and every person you play, but copying the player who just beat you may not bring the benefits you hope for.

Why not? Well, it's likely that you aren't the only one who has noticed that superhuman player at the hobby shop, the one who brags about arranging a deck to achieve a certain goal. Soon, a dozen other players may be copying all the moves used by this supposed expert. This means your strategy may be recognized by opponents who are trying the same plan.

Meanwhile, the winner everyone admires keeps winning. That's because top players keep experimenting with new decks. Their old strategies often disappear.

So, how do they keep winning? They might tell you it's a special card, making you want that card. But did the card win the game, or was it when the card was played? Does a card win a game, or does the person who played it?

## Learn from the Experts

Some players think practice is the best way to beat these common problems. Yet, watching without playing can be nearly as helpful. In a two-person game, ask both players if you can watch (without interrupting or giving one player clues, of course). After the match, advanced gamers will probably be flattered if you ask their opinions. Like sports announcers, they can give you their views on why one player won and the other lost, along with how different strategies could have changed the outcome.

When you get beaten by a more experienced player, don't be shy about asking for advice. Everyone was a beginner once. After all, collectible card games haven't been around forever.

Ask if your deck may have some ineffective cards. What helpful cards could be added? Many players will be honest if you ask them why you lost.

Why would an opponent tell you a secret technique? You'll understand if you've taught any of your friends to play. Wouldn't it be nice to feel that you started the career of a future champion? "I taught her that move!" you could proudly claim. Besides, playing a real whiz kid you've helped is more challenging for you—and more fun—than beating someone who didn't know about the game.

Sharing knowledge and discoveries with interested, interesting people is a big part of the fun. Winning is fine, but it isn't really the point. If winning were the point, we wouldn't play collectible card games—

after all, these games depend on luck. But people like CCGs because, sometimes, being lucky is as much fun as being best.

Luck is a surprise, and people like surprises. That may be why almost every country in the world has some form of the games *Hide-and-Seek* and *Blind Man's Bluff.* These games have the same surprise, a good surprise: discovering a friend.

Drawing a lucky card is a good surprise, too. And winning because you drew a lucky card lets you enjoy being the luckiest for a day. You don't have to worry about how to be lucky tomorrow—luck is just luck. Congratulate yourself for making good plans that let you use that luck. And when your friend is lucky, you can congratulate your friend on making good plans—and learn how to make new plans.

Because luck is just luck, the game stays a game, not a task with required skills, not a measure of success or failure.

## Branch Out

Remember, the first trading-card game you learn may not be the one you'll like best. You may really enjoy some aspects of that first game and simply tolerate other parts. So learn another game—and another. You'll find the right combination that becomes the game you enjoy. That's the real victory.

Within months after *Magic: The Gathering* became a hit, other companies tried making card games with different themes and story lines, to widen players' choices. Here are some of the first alternative games. This list won't tell you which games are "good" or "bad." It will show you the many different subjects that became playing material in the early days of CCGs.

*Dixie:* Who needs to invent heroes and villains when history is stuffed full of rascals and rogues? Once, kids played *War* or *Army* and chased each other around the playground. Here's a chance to enjoy the same sort of excitement while finding out how history may have changed during America's Civil War.

*GridIron:* Published by the Upper Deck Company (well known to sports-card collectors), this football game earned the title of first sports-oriented CCG.

*Illuminati: New World Order:* For older players who read the newspaper every day, but don't take it too seriously. This game

**Time Warp**

Requires last turn to be replaye[d]
(the same cards may not be
played).

Sometimes fear and psychic energ[y]
can rip the fabric of time.

**Special**

Copyright © 1994 C[SI]
Illo © Dave Ula[...]

**+2**

**First National Bank**

Adds to each stack on your side in
the battle.

The principal repository of money in
every city.

**1**

**Yarf the Tr[oll]**

Begin super villai[n]
Awakened when hi[s]
replaced by a 6 la[...]
power comes from[...]
now destroys oth[...]
traffic on his ow[n]

**Base**
**V**

**3**

**Starflare**

Begin super hero stack[...]
An energy beam from the[...]
randomly struck Aidan Wells[...]
him super powers and a purpose[...]
preserve that future in order to[...]
preserve his powers and his life.

**Base**
**H**

Copyright © 1994 C[...]
Illo © J A [...]

**Alien Cure**

Removes any Plague, Virus, or
Epidemic.

**Special**

Copyright © 1994 CSI
Illo © John Mundt, Esq.

of political satire has been called by some "good, clean, back-stabbing fun."

*OverPower:* This game is full of battles between Marvel heroes and baddies, from Spider-Man to Venom, all with the super comic-book art you'd expect. The neatest part is that players wager cards, just for fun. Can you bluff other players into believing your hand is best?

*Rage:* Based on a role-playing game called *Werewolf,* this game has special appeal to collectors. Made by Upper Deck, two hard-to-find "chase" cards were randomly inserted into all thirty-six-count booster packs.

*Redemption:* Peopled with characters from the Bible, this game challenges players to rescue "lost souls" from the forces of darkness.

*SimCity The Card Game:* Based on a computer game, *SimCity* is more than a variation on the board game of *Monopoly.* You buy land and build an entire town on it, including schools, churches, factories, floods, and other natural disasters, even politicians. (If you don't buy your way into public office, you'd better keep on the good side of the person who does!)

*Spellfire:* From TSR, the makers of *Dungeons & Dragons* role-playing systems, this game presents the quests and fantasy of D&D with cards.

*Star Trek: The Next Generation (ST: TNG):* Assemble your spaceship and your crew and set out on missions throughout the universe.

*Star Wars:* From Decipher, the makers of *ST: TNG*, this game relies more on battles than missions. Both games use photographs from the TV and movie productions.

*SuperDeck!:* Fight two battles at once: your superhero versus your opponent's villain, and your supervillain against her hero. You have to win both battles at once in order to win the war.

*Ultimate Combat!:* These cards combine the different arts of self-defense. Can a karate move resist a wrestling hold?

*Wyvern:* Dragons and knights, and you know what that means....

## Beyond Cards

Card games have even inspired more than other card games. Within two years of its creation, *Magic: The Gathering* was issued

*Conventions are places where game enthusiasts can meet other players, participate in tournaments, sample new products, and see some of their favorite, familiar games. At the huge annual convention known as GenCon, TSR builds this castle based on its popular* Dungeons & Dragons *role-playing game.*

as a computer game. *Magic* has also become a series of novels and a series of comic books.

Other games, such as *Spellfire*, have inspired T-shirts, figurines, even poster art.

These trinkets, like carrying cases and multisided score-keeping dice, are not part of playing. They are just things that keep a player "in the mood."

The games remain the primary interest of game enthusiasts. Tournaments are held at conventions around the United States, and national and world championships are held in America and overseas, with contestants sometimes traveling halfway around the world to compete.

Game conventions are gatherings of game creators, publishers, and distributors, as well as players. These conventions, known as cons, also offer classes and discussion groups for honing players' skills. They also provide opportunities to meet artists, designers, and champions of favorite games.

New games are often previewed or introduced at conventions, giving folks who attend a chance to try a game before it hits the stores. In other words, gamers just like you get a chance to play-test a game, and become part of that game's development and history by offering comments and suggestions. Conventions also offer promotional pieces that may become rare or historical, too, if the game undergoes significant changes after the convention.

Try many different games. You'll find out what you like, but also what you don't. Both kinds of information can help you—and either one could inspire you—to create new games just for you and your friends.

Either way, you get a good deal.

# *Appendix*

# HOBBY MAGAZINES AND MORE

To keep your playing skills sharp or your collection current, it's important to keep reading. That means more than just this book. There are many sources that can aid you in your journey through the world of collectible card games.

The first stop in your travels for current information should be at least one hobby magazine. The many choices include:

*Conjure* (2272 Kresge Drive, Amherst, OH 44001). This magazine started out more expensive than competitors. Large type, lots of illustrations, and the basics of game reviews and strategy hints make this a decent "starter" publication.

*Cons Unlimited* (P.O. Box 1740, Renton, WA 98057). This newspaper is a freebie to anyone attending a games convention. Subscriptions are available at a low cost. This provides a great introduction to what you can expect when attending a con, even if you can't make the upcoming events detailed in each issue. (If the address looks familiar, it's because Wizards of the Coast acquired the gaming-industry-convention management company in early 1995.)

*The Duelist* (P.O. Box 707, Renton, WA 98057-0707). Because this magazine is owned by Wizards of the Coast (WotC), it centers around the company's products, with other CCGs duly noted. *The Duelist* is a leader in creating helpful how-to articles, such as "Solitaire Magic" and "Trading to Win: Strategies from the World Champion," along with an array of playing-strategy tips.

Although single copies of *The Duelist* can be purchased at game shops and newsstands, there's a better option. A yearly membership in The Duelists' Convocation qualifies you for the quarterly magazine, *The Duelists' Companion* newsletter (sent in months you don't receive the magazine), and the right to play in official WotC-approved tournaments. Tourney players can earn points to be included in national rankings.

*Game Shop News* (1266 West Paces Ferry Rd., #455, Atlanta, GA 30327). This tabloid can't match the colorful, glossy appeal of magazines, but it is given out for free by many shops to reward loyal customers. If you can't find *GSN*, ask your card dealer about it. Includes interviews and game tips.

*InQuest* (Wizard Press, 151 Wells Ave., Congers, NY 10920-2064). Most of each issue of this magazine is new-product news and a price guide. However, early issues displayed a willingness to win over beginning and intermediate gamers with eye-opening features such as "A Beginner's Guide to Building a Winning Magic Deck," "History of Role-Playing Games," and "How to Break into Gaming (as a Game Designer)."

*Scrye* (30617 U.S. Highway 19 North, Suite 700, Palm Harbor, FL 34684). Call this the grandparent of the hobby-magazine family. *Scrye* has an ideal mix of new product news, checklists, in-depth game reviews and histories, tournament updates, and the hobby's most reliable price guide. The magazine serves readers everywhere by providing regional dealer reports. This way, if you live in Idaho, for example, you can find out what's happening in game shops in other parts of the country.

*Ventura* (1920 Highland Ave., Suite 222, Lombard, IL 60148). *Ventura* comes from the makers of *Hero Illustrated*. *Ventura* rivals *Scrye* with an excellent mix of in-depth articles reflecting every facet of CCGs.

# Write for More Info

Most companies are willing to stay in touch with their playing customers, answer questions, and provide lists of frequently asked questions (FAQs) from other gamers. You can communicate by mail or by computer.

If you're looking for players who share your interests, on-line opportunities exist. No matter what computer service you subscribe to, there may be bulletin boards or interest groups to investigate.

Once you discover information, don't let it go to waste. Share it—that's what games are for.

Mailing and on-line addresses (when available) for several games and their producers are listed here. They are arranged alphabetically by company name; the game name appears in italics at the top of each listing. If the company is not listed here, you should be able to find its address (for e-mail, too) listed in instructions in starter decks and booster pack wrappers, as well as in hobby magazines.

*On the Edge:*
Atlas Games
P.O. Box 131233
Roseville, MN 55113
e-mail:
 buford@winternet.
 com/atlas@io.com

*Tempest of the Gods:*
Black Dragon Press
P.O. Box 362
Logan, UT 83705
e-mail:
 bdpress1@aol.com

*Redemption:*
Cactus Game
 Designs
1553 South Military
 Highway
Chesapeake, VA 23320
e-mail:
 cactusrob@aol.com

*Powercardz:*
Caliber Game Systems
11918 Farmington Rd.
Livonia, MI 48150

*SuperDeck!:*
Card Sharks Inc.
1418 North Clinton Blvd.
Bloomington, IL 61701
e-mail:
 cardsharks@aol.com

*Hyborian Gates:*
Cardz
2505 North Highway 360,
7th Floor
Grand Prairie, TX 75050
e-mail:
 hyborian@aol.com

*Dixie:*
Columbia Games Inc.
P.O. Box 3457
Blaine, WA 98231
e-mail:
  cgi/94@aol.com

*Star Quest:*
Comic Images
280 Midland Ave.
Saddle Brook, NJ 07663
e-mail:
  starquest@nic.com

*Chrysalis:*
Comico
119 West Hubbard,
  4th Fl.
Chicago, IL 60610

*Galactic Empires:*
Companion Games
P.O. Box 392
Stamford, NY 12167
e-mail:
  cmpanion@nyc.
  pipeline.com

*Shadowfist:*
Daedalus Games
P.O. Box 880
Mercer Island, WA
98040-0880
e-mail:
  fisttrade
  request@mars.
  galstar.com
  (for e-mail list)

*Shadowfist, continued:*
  robmh@aol.com
  (for questions)

*Star Trek, Star Wars:*
Decipher Inc.
253 Granby St.
Norfolk, VA 23510-1813
e-mail:
  dcustserve@aol.com

*Top of the Order,*
*Red Zone:*
Donruss
2355 Waukegan Road
Bannockburn, IL 60015
e-mail:
  nxtgames@cts.com

*Flights of Fantasy:*
Destini Products Inc.
73 Fessenden St.
Warwick, RI 02886

*Overpower* and all *Marvel* games:
Fleer
1120 Route 73
Mt. Laurel, NJ 08054

*Guardians:*
FPG
2539 Washington Rd.,
  Building 1000
Pittsburgh, PA 15241
e-mail:
  joefpg@aol.com

*Doomtrooper:*
Heartbreaker Hobbies
260 East Woodland Ave.
Springfield, PA 19064

*Middle-Earth:*
Iron Crown
    Enterprises
P.O. Box 1605
Charlottesville, VA
 22902
e-mail:
    metwice@aol.com

*Realms Arcana:*
Knight Press
264 Main St.
Florence, KY 41042

*Heresy:*
Last Unicorn Games
P.O. Box H
New Cumberland, PA
 17070
e-mail:
    monomyth@aol.com

*Star of the Guardians:*
Mag Force 7
P.O. Box 1106
Williams Bay, WI
 53191
e-mail:
    dperrin@wise
    net.com

*SimCity The Card Game:*
Mayfair Games Inc.
5641 Howard St.
Niles, IL 60714
e-mail:
    fprice@interaccess.com

*Echelons of Fire, Fire:*
Medallion Simulations
9439 North Saybrook,
    Suite 257
Fresno, CA 93720
e-mail:
    pelagis@aol.com

*Battlelords:*
New Millennium
P.O. Box 12582
Albany, NY 12212-2582
e-mail:
    NMEGames@aol.com

*Moons of Khadar:*
Outer Earth Inc.
5996 Northeast Haystack St.
Hillsboro, OR 97124

*GridIron:*
Precedence Publishing
P.O. Box 28397
Tempe, AZ 85281
e-mail:
    gridiron@eternity.com

*Illuminati:*
*New World Order:*
Steve Jackson Games
P.O. Box 18957
Austin, TX 78760
e-mail:
    sjgames@io.com

*Highlander,*
*Towers in Time:*
Thunder Castle Games
P.O. Box 11529
Kansas City, MO 64138
e-mail:
    highlander-1-
    request@netcom.com
or  towers-1-
    request@netcom.com
(for e-mail list)
    vjmurphy@net
    com.com
    or tcgames@aol.com
    (for questions)

*Blood Wars, Spellfire:*
TSR
Dragon Publishing
P.O. Box 756
Lake Geneva, WI 53147
e-mail:
    tsrinc@aol.com

*Ultimate Combat:*
Ultimate Games
2211 Moorpark Ave.
    Suite 280
San Jose, CA 95128
e-mail:
    davelong@aol.com
    or shimban@
    ultimategames.com

*Wyvern:*
U.S. Games Systems Inc.
179 Ludlow St.
Stamford, CT 06902
e-mail:
    usgames@aol.com

*Rage, Vampire: The*
*Eternal Struggle:*
White Wolf
780 Park North Blvd.,
    Suite 100
Clarkston, GA 30021
e-mail:
    ragecom@aol.com

*WildStorms:*
WildStorm
888 Prospect St., Suite 240
LaJolla, CA 92037

*Magic: The Gathering,*
*Vampire:*
Wizards of the Coast
P.O. Box 707
Renton, WA 98057-0707
e-mail:
   mtg-1@wizards.com
   (for e-mail list)
   questions@
   wizards.com
   (for questions)
   vtes-1@wizards.com
   (for questions
   about *Vampire*)

GAMA (Games Manufacturers Association)
P.O. Box 602
Swanton, OH 43558
Telephone: 1-419-826-GAMA
   e-mail: stellarlc@aol.com

GAMA is a nonprofit trade association made up of manufacturers, store owners, magazine publishers, card makers, and others in the business of CCGs and other games. Contact GAMA if you can't find a certain card company's address, or if you need help finding out if your favorite company has e-mail. Tell teachers, librarians, and parents that GAMA sponsors a newsletter "by educators, for educators," telling how collectible card games are used in the classroom and other teaching situations.

# Glossary

Just because people play the same games doesn't mean they speak the same language. Here are some terms commonly used in the world of games.

*Ante* (pronounced ANT-ee)—When playing for ante, you draw a card from your opponent's deck before the game begins, and she draws a card from yours. These cards are set aside and not played in the match. Whoever wins keeps the ante cards. In the game of marbles, this is called "playing for keeps."

*Booster*—Small packs of cards, but not enough to play with by themselves. The cost per card is higher than it is in starter decks. Collectors are often convinced that boosters contain cards not available in other kinds of packages. Some companies deny the practice and insist that distribution of all cards is random. See also *Chase card.*

*CCG*—Abbreviation for collectible card game.

*Chase Card*—A card, printed in smaller numbers than others, which is advertised as being available only in certain kinds of packages. Some companies only provide odds of finding the chase card, such as "1 in every 36 packs." Even with the odds, the company doesn't guarantee you'll find the card. Hence, the name. Chase cards aren't considered part of the standard set.

*Collectible Card Game*—Also known as a trading card game, customizable card game, and gaming cards.

*Collector*—Someone who'll try to acquire every card in a game's set, but may not actually play the game.

*Common*—The easiest cards of a set to find. Often, these cards have less power or fewer uses in a game.

*Con*—Abbreviation for convention, an event in which cards and other games are bought, sold, and traded by collectors and dealers, where companies meet the public, and where gaming tournaments are held.

*Condition*—Term used to describe the degree to which a card is worn or damaged. A card in mint condition is brand new; a card in poor condition may be torn, worn, and bent. Other terms describing condition are: near mint, very fine, fine, very good, good, and fair. These terms help collectors buy and trade fairly.

*Counter*—1. These are markers placed on cards to indicate how much the card's power has been altered. Often they are clear colored pebbles of glass or plastic, also called tokens. 2. Multisided dice with numbers instead of dots. Some players use these to keep track of points they've gained and lost; others use plastic pebbles, pennies, paper and pencil, or anything that works.

*Deck*—An assortment of cards organized for play, usually a minimum of forty.

*Draw*—A draw is taking a new card from the top of the deck. The cards to be drawn are face down in the deck, so that only the player who draws the card will see what it is.

*Edition*—1. A single print run of cards. 2. A general term meaning any card from a certain series or printing.

*Exclusive*—A promo card that is available only through a single source, such as a magazine or convention giveaway.

*Expansion*—A subset of new cards designed for use with an old game.

*Factory-collated Set*—A complete set, sometimes containing specially made bonus cards, which is sorted and packaged by the CCG company.

*FAQ*—Abbreviation for Frequently Asked Question. Companies compile and update questions frequently asked by players and customers and share this information with the public. Answers to FAQs can often be obtained by contacting the company via phone, mail, or e-mail. FAQ answers may also be included in hobby magazines.

*Gamer*—Slang term for a player or someone who enjoys the game. A gamer may not be a collector.

*GenCon*—This is one of the hobby's oldest, most established gaming conventions, held yearly in Milwaukee, Wisconsin.

*Hand*—The number of cards (often seven) held by a player during one turn.

*Limited*—A version of a card-game set made only in a specific, limited quantity.

*Out-of-print*—A card or card game no longer made or issued by a company.

*Player's Guide*—A detailed book of rules that is printed or approved by the company that produced the cards.

*Power*—1. How useful a card is. 2. The specific numbered rating on a card, telling how many points you can score against an opponent when you make an attack. See also *Strength*.

*Promo*—This type of card is a sample, given away free in magazines or at cons. A promo may also be a preview of a card game that has not yet been released. See also *Exclusive*.

*Rare*—Cards printed in very small quantities and usually very hard to find. Some companies make even fewer "ultra-rare" cards.

*Rating*—1. The ranking of a card, compared to others in the set, based on that card's usefulness in the game. 2. The national rankings of players who compete in many tournaments.

*Reissue*—An additional printing, or new expansion, of a card or game that has not been available for a while.

*Revised*—These are cards that have been printed before, but are printed again with small changes, such as a new border, to distinguish them from the cards in the original edition.

*Role-playing Game* (RPG)—Not to be confused with a collectible card game, an RPG is a type of make-believe game. Players work together to tell a story, instead of trying to defeat each other. Players are assigned numbers that give them power in certain areas of the game, and these numbers are used to solve "problems" in the story.

*Sanctioned*—Describes an official tournament, approved by the company that makes the card game that will be played.

*Single*—An individual card from a set.

*Solitaire*—A card game for only one player.

*Stand-alone*—These expansion cards are related to a game, but can be played alone, without any of the original game's cards. *Ice Age* cards, for example, can be used with *Magic: The Gathering* cards or played alone.

*Starter*—Often a 60-card, sealed, boxed assortment from a set, offering an affordable way to start collecting and playing. Sometimes starter contents are "ready-to-play," sometimes not.

*Strength*—The number that tells, in points, the amount of damage a card can cause or what abilities a card has when "attacking" an opponent. See also *Power.*

*Theme Deck*—A deck that a player arranges to accomplish one strategy. For example, a "weenie deck" uses common cards played in combination for small, constant attacks and good defense.

*Token*—See *Counter.*

*Two-player Game*—A competition played between only two people.

*Trading Card Game*—A term favored by those who play with rather than collect cards. See *Collectible Card Game.*

*Toughness*—See *Weakness.*

*Tournament*—A series of matches held among numerous players, much like a sporting event. Losers are eliminated, and the winners compete against each other until the final winner is declared the champion.

*Uncommon*—A card that is somewhat easy to find, but has been printed in lesser quantities than the common cards of the set.

*Unlimited*—A version of a card set, often distinguished by a unique border, which will be reprinted repeatedly. Unlimited versions of a set are usually issued after the limited edition, which is offered for a shorter time in small quantities.

*Weakness*—Also called "toughness." Usually, the second number on a card tells its limitations—for example, the 3 on a 2/3 card. An opponent needs 3 points of strength to defeat a 2/3 card. These are the number of points available to defend against an attack.

# Index

# About the Authors

Thomas S. Owens and Diana Star Helmer live, write, and tell stories from their home in Marshalltown, Iowa.

Thomas Owens is the author of Millbrook's *Collecting Baseball Cards, Collecting Baseball Memorabilia,* and *Collecting Comic Books.* Diana Star Helmer is a freelance writer and the author of *Belles of the Ballpark.*

Yes, they are married.

# *Free*
# CARD OFFER

See what the excitement is all about! Receive a free card from Fantasy Adventures™, the collectible card game filled with dragons, griffins, and art by today's premier fantasy artists, and from SimCity® The Card Game™, the city-building collectible card game for the whole family.

To get your free cards, send a STAMPED, SELF-ADDRESSED ENVELOPE AND PROOF OF PURCHASE (cash register receipt attached to this coupon) to:

Mayfair Games
P.O. Box 48717
Niles, IL 60714-0717

Offer expires 3/31/97.

Fantasy Adventures is a trademark of Mayfair Games. All rights reserved. SimCity is a registered trademark of Maxis, Inc. Used Under License. SimCity® The Card Game™ is a trademark of Mayfair Games. All rights reserved.

Name _____

Address _____

City _____ State _____ Zip _____

Daytime Phone # _____

Offer expires 3/31/97. No copies of coupon or cash receipt accepted. Millbrook.